T0068039

'RISeN'
HE DIDN'T HAVE
TO DO IT
BUT HE DID IT
ANYWAY

'RISEN'
HE DIDN'T HAVE
TO DO IT
BUT HE DID IT
ANYWAY

THE LIFE STORY OF
ROYAL CHATMAN

ROYAL CHATMAN

authorHOUSE®

AuthorHouse™
1663 Liberty Drive
Bloomington, IN 47403
www.authorhouse.com
Phone: 1-800-839-8640

Published by AuthorHouse   10/02/2012

ISBN: 978-1-4772-7577-1 (sc)
ISBN: 978-1-4772-7578-8 (e)

Library of Congress Control Number: 2012918394

CONTENTS

I would Like To Thank God First For allowing Me To Overcome all Obstacles that tried To Hinder Me From Writing this Testimony, I would Like To Thank My Loving Wife who has been a Heaven sent For Her Support and Bringing Life to the Final Chapter of the Book. I give a Special Thanks to Dan & Myrna Willmouth Who was the soul Foundation of Making Sure the Book Was Complete. Myrna has Truly Place Her Heart and Soul into Making sure the edit Part of the Book was Perfect Her. Patience with Me was Truly A Blessing and I Would Like to Thank Pastor Gregg and His Wife Sharrah and the Victory Church Family Who has Shared Nothing But The Love of God Since We Found Our Place in the Fold.

CHAPTER 1

THE JEREMIAH STAGE

Jeremiah 29:11 "For I know the plans I have for you," says the LORD. "They are plans for good and not for disaster, to give you a future and a hope." NLT

Jeremiah 1:19 "They will fight you, but they will fail. For I am with you, and I will take care of you. I, the LORD have spoken."

The purpose in writing this book is to humble myself and give thanks to the Lord, who has allowed me to continue breathing His precious gift of life. You will have a better understanding of why I say these things, when you read this book in its entirety.

I remember so clearly my coming of age. I was a teenager, and, like all other energized kids, I was out to have fun every living moment. Well, I tried my best to enjoy each day—at least until the street lights came on at night. So vivid in my mind is the day my neighbor's grandson, Gary, was out painting his auntie's house, and he asked me if I would like to help. The fact that he would pay me made this a no "brainer," because we were talking about the penny candy store days. To get a kid's attention quickly was to let him know that money was being given, so I was all for this deal. Never did I suspect that the Lord had much more in store than money for some penny candy.

When we got to the house that was to be painted, there was a long ladder resting against the roof. It seemed to reach to heaven, which was scary to this kid in case I had to climb the thing and paint. By this time, the penny candy wasn't looking to be too necessary. Then Gary said, "All you have to do is hold the ladder while I am on it and hand me a paint brush." Those words were joy to my ears and once again the excitement of buying the penny candy returned.

As he was painting he began to ask me about school. I told him how, at times, I would get upset with the kids that made jokes about my clothes or shoes with holes. He said, "You should come with me to A.Y.F." I, of course, asked him what it was and he told me it was an Adult Youth Fun Bible study. This information did not seem to move me with a quick response. You know what I thought to myself, "Oh, no, here we go again with some more kids to make fun of me—and adults too this time." Those thoughts flew out the window as he replied that we all get together and have fun playing games, going to the park, playing basketball and air hockey. Also, he said they had Bible study and ordered pizza. That did it! Pizza and I was all ears. He asked me about my siblings and if they would like to come. Even though I admitted I had three brothers and one sister, I didn't want to include them. I felt the less people that were there, the more pizza I could have.

When I mentioned there was another sister, part of triplets, that died at birth, he looked down at me holding that ladder and spoke some powerful words, "You can see your sister again." These words changed my life; however, at the time I thought he was making a joke. I asked, "How can I see her again when I have never seen her in the first place?" Gary asked me if I had ever heard the name Jesus, and I had not. Then he told me that I must get saved and I would be able to see my sister, because she was with Jesus and that all who were saved will see Him, and see those who died in Him. Now this was the beginning of my wanting to know more about this man named Jesus. I continued to listen to him as he finished painting, and I made a decision to go to A.Y.F.

A.Y.F. was really fun, but I must admit the pizza was the best part. Yes, it should have been the Bible study, but, come on, I was a teenager with a menu of fun, food and pizza on my mind. As I began to question Gary more about Jesus and how I would be able to see my dead sister if I died saved, the more I wanted to learn. Some nights after A.Y.F. I would go home and tell my mother I wanted to die, if I was saved, so I could see my sister, Tamara. My mother would get mad and tell me not to talk about such matters. She asked me who had been telling me all this stuff. I told her about my friend, Gary. Then she exclaimed, "I don't want you going no more with them and filling your head with crazy mess about Tamara and now you wanting to die makes me mad." It was my turn to get mad now and crying and telling Mom how much I wanted to keep attending, that she was being unfair and the whole nine yards. She finally agreed if I would stop talking about seeing my sister and dying. I agreed. What amazed me then, and still does to this day, is that she never denied me talking about the man named Jesus.

My goal from that point on was to get to know Him, seeing that He was the one I needed to know in order to see my sister. Thinking back, it was funny because the more I went to the fun and study time, the more I learned and the more I showed up at school. It did not hurt as much when the kids made jokes about my pop belly and big eyes, and their laughing at me did not seem to bother me as much. I must admit there was a change going on, but, at that point, I could not quite make sense of it all.

Summer vacation break from school was just around the corner. Gary invited me to a planned yearly trip to a Christian camp in Canada. I was fifteen now and as my brothers and sister and any young kid, I loved summer break with no school and all fun. I knew little about Christians and how could camp be as much fun as spending time with the kids on my block. Nevertheless, that urging was there, so I begged my mother for permission to go and some money for the trip. Reluctantly, she said yes and gave me the money I needed to join. I was shocked as she did not hesitate.

At camp, there were kids from all over the United States, so I expected some laughing and joking at my expense. The first morning we broke up into groups and had all types of activities. Later in the day we would all join together for songs and studies. Even I had to admit there were lots of fun things to do. We had horseback riding, swimming lessons, ping pong, basketball and arts and crafts. One thing I found so interesting was the drama and skits that were themes about Jesus. This really drew me because once again there was the Name I was trying to get to know more about. Naturally, this was the area I spent most of my time.

I remember one night we were all together, and the leaders divided us into semi-large groups to ask us if we had any habits or addictions. I was puzzled for a moment, until they began to give us some examples, such as cigarettes, drugs and gambling. The light bulb went off for me because I enjoyed shooting craps (dice). I would always find myself taking the money earned for cutting lawns, raking leaves or shoveling snow and go to the park to play dice, usually losing more than I would win. My hand went up in the air, and the leader asked, "Are you saved?" Another puzzle ran through my thoughts. I answered, "I don't know, but I have heard a lot about Jesus and my little sister was with Him now." Her next question was something like did I want to be saved and break free of the addiction of gambling. I responded that yes I did and repeated her words. At the end I asked this man named Jesus to become my Lord and forgive me for my sins. She then prayed that the Holy Spirit of the Lord would exchange my gambling desire for an upset stomach, whenever I wanted to gamble and stir up my stomach if I chose to gamble.

I tell you something happened to me that night that is unexplainable. As a kid, I began to cry, I mean cry deeply. I felt this indescribable heat, and my heart and legs felt weak at the same time. The lady leader just held me in her arms, as I literally soaked her shirt with my tears and sweat. That was the beginning of my salvation road. Gary had heard about it through the camp talk, and he was so glad for me. Soon the vacation came to an end, and it was time to go back home. For the oddest reason, the person I was when I went to camp was not the person now headed home. There was something different and new; I just could not figure out what it was.

After returning home, there was little time before we were on our way back to school. Nothing had changed the fact that the vacation was over for the summer, but a fact that had changed was something inside of me. I used to run with a neighborhood gang or more accurately tried to run with them. I was not their favorite choice, so I more or less would hang around uninvited trying to be cool. The strange thing was that after I came back from camp, I stopped even trying to hangout with them and do some of the things they did. Even weirder was the fact they started trying to get me to join them. I denied many times, until this guy named Chris began to hang out with the gang. Now I liked Chris and had seen him from time to time. Of course, he would tell me what was happening on the streets. I warned him that this stuff was not being cool and to get away from these guys, because someone was going to get hurt. Chris would always say, "It ain't that bad man." Besides he had a pocket full of money most of the time. I was pretty sure it wasn't earned mowing lawns!

The last night I saw Chris he had gone out with the guys, and his initiation into the gang was to rob somebody. It didn't matter who it was as long as he could show the

6

crew that he had guts or heart to do it. Chris saw this guy at the gas station getting gas for his moped bike. This looked like an easy opportunity; the guy was not that big and didn't look like he would put up a fight. So Chris went up to this guy, punched him in the face, grabbed the moped and rode it all over the neighborhood that night, showing off and bragging. All the crew took turns riding it. I must admit I really wanted to ride that moped; even though, I knew it was wrong. Then I saw Chris across the street at the Crawford's house, and he called my name to come over there. I couldn't wait and before my foot could reach the bottom step of our porch, I had a sudden urge to go to the bathroom. I called to Chris I would be right back.

That night seemed pretty much the same as every other Saturday night, but that was about to change. Loud words, three or four loud pops that sounded like firecrackers, people screaming and I wondered what was happening as I sat safely in the bathroom. As soon as I could, I ran down the stairs and as I reached the porch I heard words like, "Oh, my God! Why did they do that?" It did not dawn on me to look across the street, because I was watching everyone crying, screaming, yelling, and running the other direction. Finally, I turned and looked to see my friend, Chris, lying on the corner where I last saw him standing and talking with two girls. I still didn't realize what had happened, until someone shouted, "They shot him." It all became too clear why my friend was lying on the corner of the street. I raced off the porch to cross the street. My mother was calling my name but I did not hear. All I remember was the sound like a water hose slowly running water on the ground. Then my mother grabbed me from behind. As I began to cry, the thought slammed in my head that I had wanted so much to ride that moped and was within seconds of standing right there beside Chris when he was shot. My mom just held me and told me how sorry she was for my friend.

Chris had been shot two or three times in the head—the water was blood and the firecrackers were gun shots, and the loud words were from the guy Chris had punched in the face and robbed and thought would not put up much of a fight. Well, he wasn't a fighter, he was a killer. He, his brothers, and crew had been out all night looking for the guy who stole the moped and, yes, they had found him.

I knew I didn't want to have anything to do with gangs or crews anymore. I was, also, left wondering about the sudden urge to go to the bathroom at just the moment I would probably have been killed as well. After all the commotion died down and the police and the coroner vehicles left, I joined my family on the porch. They were talking about all that had happened and for some odd reason, my mother's husband, not my father, said to me, "You will not see the age of twenty-two because of the friends you have." Later still, my mother came out and saw me crying and asked why. I repeated what he had said. She really went off on him and told me, "Yes, you will baby; you will live a long time." Nevertheless, the bad, not good seed, was planted and all I could think about was just hoping to live to see twenty-two.

CHAPTER 2

BORN FATHERLESS—FACED WITH LIVING MOTHERLESS

Job 1:21 "I came naked from my mother's womb,
and I will be naked when I leave. The LORD
gave me what I had, and the Lord has taken it
away, Praise the name of the LORD!" NIV

Years had passed and I was working at the neighborhood barbecue restaurant making some money to do a few things growing teenagers like to do, such as going to the movies and shopping. The main reason though was to take a load off my mother, as I was the eldest brother. My sister was a few years older but I wanted to help. I was not hanging around those guys that caused my friend, Chris, to get killed; however, my brother D seemed to be following the wrong, nonproductive path. He found other means of making money than working, and this caused a riff between us. We would get in heated arguments many times. It seemed like he would get away with anything. I felt the least favorite of my grandmother, where we were living at the time. I really mean that to me it seemed my other brothers and sister could do anything and have anything. On the other hand, I was always told no you can't go or I would be punished for things I didn't say or do. For instance, on Saturday, I would have to clean the house, while the others got to go out and play. It all came to a head when my brother D and I really had some bad words between us, because I knew he was doing things that were not right. I knew my mother and grandmother had an idea but they never said anything, and this was very unfair.

The result was my going to live with my Auntie Barbara. It was also a changing point in my life—new school, new friends, all sorts of new people and places. Being in a different place was fun. I was still finding out more about the new feelings I experienced at summer camp and the man named Jesus. Physical changes were happening like my eyes were not as big and girls were talking to me more now. Okay, what I am trying to say in some non arrogant way is I was becoming handsome and that was cool! I wanted so much to graduate because my mother did not get the chance, as she had to drop out of school to take care of us. Then her hopes that my oldest sister would graduate didn't work out, because my sister had a child. My brother D had already chosen a path that had nothing to do with school.

One of my greatest wishes now for my mother was to see me graduate; particularly, since she was likely to become more and more ill. She had been diagnosed with breast cancer and was in remission, but another doctor visit had changed all that and she was sick again. Still I was driven to graduate and, believe me, this was not an easy thing. I was distracted at this new school, Henry Ford High, a school known for who dressed the best and who was the most popular. Of course, I was now fitting into this lifestyle. As I mentioned already, I was not the same person that used to be teased about my looks; I had different features now and I was looking good. The girls gave me some attention, and you know every school boy loves attention from the ladies. I had to stay focused on homework and classwork, if I still intended to graduate for my mom.

Meanwhile, my mother's cancer had spread, and she was in the hospital all the time. As the end of the school year was approaching, I somehow managed to be on the graduation roll call. I was happy because my mother would finally be able to know that one of her kids graduated. On the other hand, I was sad about the fact that she was sick and dying, and there was nothing the doctors could do about it. Another blow came when I was informed that she was so ill she might not be able to attend my graduation and see me receive my diploma. Talk about pain and hurt—my world became that much smaller.

On the day of my graduation, I prepared myself to go. My aunt and I were very disappointed that my mother probably would not make it. At the graduation, I was looking at all the other kids, all dressed up in their brown and gold caps and gowns. We all looked the same but I was missing that special presence that they had—they had mothers and fathers there and I didn't. The consolation that I made it would have to be enough. As I was sitting there with my peers waiting for our names to be called, my aunt called out to me, pointing up in the stands. There she was, my mother, and her husband, Chuck, the one

I would call my dad. She was wearing an oxygen mask and carrying a tank. But she had insisted the doctors let her come and see her son walk across the stage. In spite of all the pain and sickness she felt, she made them get her ready to see me get my diploma. I had the biggest smile on my face and the biggest tears in my eyes seeing her sitting there. After the cap tossing in the air, I tried to find my mother and Chuck, but my auntie told me she had to return to the hospital. Mother had also told her to tell me that nothing would have kept her from seeing me walk across that stage and receive that diploma.

The class of '88 was a great time and a great year, but January 10, 1989 was not so great. We were all called to the hospital and given the news that the doctors were going to have to take my mother off the machine. That was never the phone call I wanted to get. I recall getting there and all the family were crying and seemed to be looking at me for my response. They had been waiting on me to have all the immediate family present before turning off the breathing machine. I was the last one to arrive simply because I had not fully gripped the situation. Fatherless from birth, never knowing more than his name, now about to be motherless, a fifteen year old brother on the wrong path, eleven year old twin brothers, my sister with a child, and here I was at the ripe old age of eighteen. Yes, I took my time getting to the hospital. It brings deep sadness to this day, even at this moment as I write, because I loved my mother and she was all I had to come to my rescue and defend me when everyone made jokes about me. Even my own brothers and sister would tease me that I was adopted, because I was a shade darker than them. It was my mom that made me feel loved and special and, in the end, endured so much pain just to see me walk across a stage. Now it seemed to be only me, and I felt abandoned.

Then the oddest feeling came over me that someone else was present, and I could not explain it. How well I remember the chaplain coming into the room and saying, "I just want you all to know that I have been with your mother throughout her stay at the hospital. And I would like to let you know that she did get saved and accepted the Lord Jesus as her Lord." With that news, I looked at my brothers' and sister's faces and they looked confused as to what or to whom the chaplain was referring. Oh, but I knew so clearly what he meant, and if my little sister was with Him, then my mother would be too. Remembering what Gary said at that Christian camp, if I was saved and knew Jesus I would see my sister and my mom again.

The doctors gave us a minute and then shut off the machine. My mother seemed to give out a noticeable sigh and her chest did not move up and down anymore. My brothers and sister began to weep loudly, and I turned toward the machine and began punching it and telling it to make her breathe again. My aunt and Chuck grabbed me and took me out into the hall. At that very moment, I felt so very alone and empty inside. My mother, my hero, my best friend, my all had just died. Who was going to protect and love me kept running through my mind, as my life took another turn. I had no idea the impact this moment would have on me in the years ahead.

CHAPTER 3

THE PRODIGAL STAGE

*Luke 15:13-15 "A few days later this younger son
packed his belongings and moved to a distant land,
and there he wasted all his money in wild living.
About the time his money ran out a great famine
swept over the land, and he began to starve. He
persuaded a local farmer to hire him, and the man
sent him into his fields to feed the pigs." NLT*

My mother had been passed for months, and the sting of
it was present every morning. I wrestled with the thoughts
of what was going to become of my younger brothers and
my sister, who was trying to take on the role of being a
mother for us. My brother, who was on the wrong path,
seemed to be doing pretty well for himself with this other
means of making money. While I was struggling with the
loss of Mother and trying to discover what assistance I
could be to my siblings, I admit I had become envious
of my brother D. Here I was the eldest brother and D
was providing for the family, including helping me. We,
nevertheless, had mended our relationship and knew we

had to come together as a close knit family. We were all we had! We were responsible for our twin brothers and our sister. It was a shame that it took the death of our mother to end our dispute.

I was still in the same frame of mind as I was in the hospital months ago. I felt alone and there was nothing anybody could tell me. We had been told that our mother had some savings bonds and life insurance. Knowing this made it seem like things were about to get a little easier. When we all got our share, I remember going out and buying a car with part of mine. My sister was in charge of my younger twin brothers' portions. As to my other brother, I felt he did not need his share, because of his lifestyle and income that outweighed the part he was getting. I had a small portion of mine in the bank, when my brother gave me a call and said we needed to talk. I agreed to meet him at our grandmother's house. If I had known where this conversation would take me, I never would have gone.

The first thing he wanted to know was if I had any money left or had I spent it all. I was hesitant to answer but, finally, told him I had some money left. Then he said, "You need to go in half with me on something." I thought he of all people didn't need money from me. Besides I felt he probably still had his full share. I replied, "What and why?" He said we had to start looking out for the family and we would be making a lot more back, because we would be in business for ourselves. Confused as I was, I listened while he began telling me or schooling me on what he does and how he makes money. I got a one on one class on selling drugs. The amounts of money we

could make by being in business for ourselves was like a drug in itself.

This was the beginning of my "prodigal" walk, as I would produce a lot more money in his way of life than in mine. Now it saddens me to say that it was a lot like the offer I got from Gary to paint his aunt's house for penny candy, only this time it was not for penny candy. I did not even give it much thought; I just agreed. I asked what I would do and he said not to worry, he would teach me. So I took the rest of my money and gave it to D. It amazes me now that I placed all I had left in the trust of my brother with little understanding of what he did and how he did it. We certainly did not always see eye to eye; yet, the thought that I had not hesitated was despairing. My choices had become numb to consequences, which should have been the first warning sign that this fork in the road of life was the wrong one. I can certainly say that I caught on to what my brother taught me very quickly. He was right—the return on the money was more than the investment and it was fast. What I would have made working two to three months, I could make in a matter of hours.

Here I was climbing up the ladder so to speak. I was shopping like crazy, eating at nice restaurants, and being recognized by the people in the business. I was the topic of conversation in our part of town, not to mention, the ladies giving me compliments. This had to be a result of the way I dressed and certainly my jewelry. Even the guys would take a double look at what my brother and I wore around our necks and on our fingers. I remember buying gym shoes every chance I got; I mean three or four pairs at a time in order to make up for all those shoes with holes the kids used to tease me about when I was young. I hated those shoes I had to wear to school in the rain and the water ran in the bottom. What I was doing was making up for lost time and lost chances. I'm not even trying to make excuses for what I was doing, because to be quite honest, after my mother died, I didn't care about me. Besides I was helping the family have things. If they couldn't have a father and mother, then they could have stuff. I was just on the wrong path and realized I was also filled with selfish ambitions.

In the meantime, I moved to the west side of Detroit, where people lived and acted differently and the whole atmosphere was better. The east side was rougher and tougher and the boys were out to get you. The west side was more laid back, so I made up my mind to stay in my part of town and let my brother have the other side. I also looked at the possibility that we could make more money by covering more territory. As things continued and my popularity increased, the deeper the hole I dug for myself. I always told myself that when I made a certain amount of money, I would quit. Well, that was a lie because the more I made the more I wanted. This lifestyle was addictive, as I was transformed from an unhappy, teased person to the one everybody wanted as a friend. Of course, I was now convinced that I was really cool!

One day I was at the Rim Shop buying rims for my car, and I was approached by a guy who was a friend of a friend. You know how that goes. He said, "I been watching you man, and I heard a lot about you and that you are not like these other guys." My antennas went up because I was sure this guy was a cop. I was a little scared

and angry at the same time. If he was a cop, I knew I was in trouble and if not a cop, then why was this guy all up in my business. Looking at the guy I told him, "You got the wrong person man, and I don't even know what you are talking about." At the same time, I am pulling $4,500 out of my pocket to pay for the rims and tires. He said we would talk later and to ask my boy, Dave, who he was. This shocked and puzzled me, because Dave was the guy I looked up to and Dave owned the Rim Shop. Later that day, Dave told me the man that approached me was not a cop but a "connect."

I remembered when my brother schooled me, he said that we would really be "on" if we ever got a "connect." So in other words, I was chosen by the man himself. Of course, I still did not know what that meant, but many things were about to change. One day when I was doing my usual thing, this car pulled up and inside was the guy that stopped me at the rim store. He had another man with him and told me to put his phone number in my phone and call him tomorrow. Following instructions, I called him and he asked me, "How many do you want?" He meant kilos and I had never seen a kilo before, and usually had just a few ounces—maybe three at the most. There are thirty-six ounces in one kilo and he was asking me how many I wanted. I knew then he really had me mixed up with someone else, because I couldn't afford half a kilo, let alone buy even one. He knew I was hesitating and said, "Man don't worry; I done talked to Dave and whatever you need I am going to front them to you. Dave said you were good people." He came over to my apartment with a gym bag and place it on the couch. Before I could tell him I could give him a certain amount of money, he said to take my time paying him the eighteen for each and left. I agreed and it dawned on me there must be more than one in the bag. I opened it and there were four kilos. Immediately I called my hommie Sean and my brother as I was not sound on the prices for this. I found out that kilos were being sold on the street for $24,000 and I had four in the bag and the guy only wanted $18,000 each.

Taking a big drink of pride knowing I could get as much as I wanted, any thought of ever turning back flew out the window. From that one phone call that day, I went from making a couple of thousand a week to $10,000 to $15,000 every three days. My head was so big and I pictured myself some sort of new age Robinhood trying to help the poor and doing all kinds of self righteous acts, thinking this would make that unhappiness and bitterness inside, that I carried from the death of my mother, go away. This all created a gap between my twin brothers and sister, because I stopped going around them. I didn't want anything to happen to them in case something went wrong in this life I had chosen. They would be okay from a distance and I checked with their school and teachers to make sure they were doing well. They had to be protected from my life and my kind of people, as I feared them being kidnapped and held for ransom or something like that.

Looking at all the money and hooking up with a "connect" that gets 500-1500 kilos every other month, I realized this environment was not safe for family or anyone for that matter. If anything goes wrong, these guys look to those closest to you, but this was the choice I had made and it was hard to break from it now. I didn't have to do it, but I did it anyway. Why am I telling you, the reader, this? It is simply because this path in my life and my choices along that path were not choices I ever thought I would even consider making. Instead of finding help and healing, I allowed anger and bitterness over my mother's death become my excuse to be this person I did not even recognize. I lived strictly on impulse never looking back, always washing out the truth that I had become what I was doing. I even made myself feel better by not selling drugs on Sunday but going to church with two pagers on my hip. One foot in the streets and one foot in church and maybe God would overlook my Monday through Saturday living.

I guess I should have learned what the Bible was talking about in the book of Galatians that God is not mocked.

> Galatians 6:7 "Do not be deceived, God is not mocked; for whatever a man sows, that he will also reap." NKJV

Little did I know that soon I would be paying the reaper. I never knew quite how much money was being made, until I got a call to sweep the streets. This meant sell no more drugs but collect all the money that is out. It got to the point, after two nights, that $1.6 million was counted, and we had to tell guys to hold what they had as we had no more room to keep it and surely no more patience to count it. That is when it dawned on me that things were really out of hand.

CHAPTER 4

THROUGH THE VALLEY OF THE SHADOW OF DEATH

Psalm 23:4 "Yea, though I walk through the valley of the shadow of death, I will fear no evil: for though art with me; thy rod and thy staff they comfort me." KJV

It was the end of the summer of 1991 and that September all seemed to be going well. Some of us had chartered a flight to Atlantic City, because we liked to get away now and then. I had to cancel the flight because a deal had been set up with this guy from out of town. I had no reason to believe this deal would be any different from the others. We would meet as always, I would get the money and he would leave town again. This time he brought somebody with him. It was the police and, yep, it was a setup!!!

After I was arrested, the reality sunk in, that untouchable lie we feed ourselves, that we will always get out and quit before we get caught, had finally caught up with me. A pin just burst that hot air balloon of lies that I told myself living in the fast lane of life. When my lawyer got to the jail, I was so naive about the law and what possibilities I was facing that I actually thought I would be able to buy myself out of this one. I really thought I had hurt no one; after all, I was not a murderer or a thief. What a surprise to learn that I could be facing natural life in prison. My heart dropped and I said, "You are joking, right?" I was thinking this was some lawyer ploy to get more money. He asked me if I had been watching the news, and I thought this was a dumb question. "I don't have time to watch the news," I told him. Then he advised me a law had just passed that if you are caught with a certain amount of drugs, with or without any priors, you received mandatory punishment which is natural life in my case. It is called the "650 lifer law." I asked him to do everything he could to get me out on bond, because I knew they would never see me again. He began to go about seeing what he could do. That is when I said, "No matter what the cost, get me out of here."

At my court appearance, he managed to get me a $50,000 cash/surety bond, and I was out of there. I guess at this point of the book, I should be telling you that while I was out on bond, I tried to straighten up my life and go to church to change my ways. Well, this is not exactly the truth, because those pagers went with me. There was just no way this twenty-two year old was going back to court and to jail for the rest of my life. Then I remembered that age and that famous number twenty-two that my mother's husband had used in his prediction. Remember the night Chris was killed and Chuck told me that I would never see that age, if I kept running with the friends I chose. Well, I had made it 22 years and was about to be locked up for the rest of my life. My mind was definitely on running and I would need lots of money. I continued doing what I knew best to get large sums of money. Being out on bond required I be much more cautious of who I sold drugs to, because I sure didn't need to be set up again.

That, however, should have been the least of my worries considering what would take place in the months to come. I recall being in church on a December Sunday morning, and the message was so clear. All I could really remember of the preacher's sermon were the words "the valley of the shadow of death." He said something to the effect that God allowed you to be taken there and let death surround you. Then God would snatch you back; then you would serve Him. Now if you knew me, I always thought the message was for the person in the next pew. So I didn't give it much thought, until I found myself in that valley of the shadow of death the following Wednesday.

It was December 3, 1992 and I awoke as any Wednesday with nothing out of the norm. My pager went off and a friend of mine was looking to purchase six kilos. He had called the night before but I was out to eat with my boy, Marco, and I didn't do any deals after dark. Marco had overheard the conversation and wanted to be with me when the deal went down. He told me something didn't feel right about the caller, and Marco had only met the guy once. I told him I didn't mind and would let him know. Later, the guy paged me to meet, and I told him it would be a few minutes. He was persistent to hurry as he had his guys in town that were buying and they wanted to get back on the road. So I was immediately on my way and didn't waste time calling Marco; even though, Marco had insisted I not go alone. It was early and I figured I would be just fine.

I arrived at this house and here we go—another turning point in my life. This life I led was about to unveil more of its real, true, ugly side. This day was what I called the day of the house of horror!!! I went in the house and was told to take a seat in the kitchen and the doors locked behind me. I did not think much of it until another guy emerged from the other room with a gun in his hand. My first thought was the police but that thought canceled very quickly, when the other one pulled out his gun, told me to get up and forced me down in the basement. He asked me where all my money and dope were stored. I soon realized they weren't buying, they wanted everything I had. There was a so called drought going on and kilos were going for $32,000 a piece. Now we always made it a point never to let anyone know where we laid our head at night, but these guys were yelling and threatening me. All I could here were those preacher's words, "If I have to take you through the valley of the shadow of death and let it surround you; then I will snatch you from it and you will serve me." These guys' lips were moving but the preacher's words were ringing in my head over and over.

Next came the most unusual sound and pain I had ever heard or felt, as the hammer that had been lying on the basement steps struck me across the face. This was followed by one of the guys saying they had to knock me out and put me in the trunk of the car. So they proceeded to punch me and beat me in the head with a two by four and the hammer. The pain was horrific and then, the strangest thing, something inside of me refused to see this being my death. I don't know what came over me, but I just exclaimed, "Man, stop beating me and I will get in the trunk." Would you believe they stopped? They took me to the bottom of the steps and looking up, I saw the most beautiful sight I presently thought I would never see again—I saw the sunshine outside. I remember telling the Lord that I had rather be shot outside than in this basement or in the trunk of a car, where this type of killing ended up being set on fire.

I was overwhelmed with the feeling that in spite of all these supposed to be friends and all my family that said they loved me, no one could be there to save me. As I was going up the stairs, someone threw a jacket over my face because I was bleeding profusely. I snatched the jacket off my head and threw it on the floor in case I could see any opportunity of escape. So as I was being led up, me in between these two guys, the guy in front reached into his waist and pulled out his gun. Then he passed it to the guy behind me, and this guy stopped and placed the gun about a couple of inches from my head. Then he said the words to the guy in front that broke me mentally, "Do you want me to do him here or there?" Now that meant to shoot me and from where he had the gun, that would have been the last sound I ever heard. Then the other guy said, "No, we are going to do him there!!!!!" This still did not bring me comfort mentally, because it was plain they were going to kill me. So, as we reached the top of the steps, which were right at his side door, I was faced with seeing the trunk of my car open right at the door a few steps out. Now to the average person these were only supposed to be used to store spare tires and jumper cables or a few miscellaneous items. Today, all I could see was a casket on wheels.

My moment of escape came when one guy headed to the driver's door and the other was behind me with the gun trying to throw me in the trunk. As he bear hugged me, I grabbed the back of his legs and pushed all my weight backwards causing him to fall with me on top of him. I wrestled for his gun and all the time he was punching me in the face. An unexplainable charge came over me and not even feeling his punches, I almost had my hand around the handle of the gun, fully intending to pull the trigger. Then there was a thump and great throbbing on the top of my head, as the other guy hit me with the two by four. The guy I had been wrestling with now held the gun to my cheek. As I pushed to get up and run, he pushed the gun into the bottom of my jaw and pulled the trigger.

All I could remember was the loud ringing in my ears—I mean loud—and coughing and the intense heat on the left side of my face. I began to run from the side of his house determined to live. In spite of the fact that there was a spray mist coming from the right side of my face, it had not occurred to me that I had been shot in the left side of my jaw. The harder I ran the more the spray. I ran a block to the car wash where I was well known, and they took me in, making sure nobody was following me, grabbed towels and tried to stop the bleeding. The owner said, "Man, they shot you twice." I said there had just been one shot, and he informed me I had two holes. It then hit me that the bullet went in the left side of my face and came out on the right side of my neck.

My friends got me to the hospital and while I didn't die, something in me truly died that day. The person that went in the hospital was not the one that left the hospital. So many questions raced in my mind. How did I get to this point in my life? Why did I take this path to a point of no return? How had I taken the little I had in the pursuit of happiness, I thought, and run the fast track not so much to wealth as to near death. I knew that no matter how much I wanted to see my mother and sister, Tamara, that I was not ready for death. I wanted to live and get to know more about the One who kept me alive, when all odds were against me and I should have been dead. The first place I would start looking would be the last place I was before that terrible day. That place to look was where I heard that preacher. I knew completely that he wasn't talking to someone in the other pew; the truth was he was talking to me. I was the one who had seen up close and personal what the valley of the shadow of death looked like. Now it was time for me to get up close and truly personal with the One who had snatched me out of its grip. I was snatched from death but I surely knew nothing about serving Him.

CHAPTER 5

THE JONAH STAGE

Jonah 2:1-2 "Then Jonah prayed to the LORD his God from inside the fish. He said, 'I cried out to the LORD in my great trouble' . . ."

Jonah 2:6-7 ". . . But you, O LORD my God snatched me from the jaws of death! As my life was slipping away, I remembered the LORD . . ."

Jonah 2:10 "Then the LORD ordered the fish to spit Jonah out onto the beach." NLT

There were definitely some changes after the shock of that ordeal. Being nearly killed did not set well with me. I even wrestled with the idea of revenge. Yes, I mean I had the urge to get back at these guys who should have been friends. To them my life had no value, but trying to get even and make them suffer just would not play out. My heart was different and I couldn't fight the fact that I was finished with the lifestyle of selling drugs. This was strange; it was as though they had shot the drug dealer straight out of me. With my court date coming up, I had to weigh the consequences of my next actions. There was still this guy out there who had shot me and he should pay for what he had done. On the other hand I was in search of the One who had snatched me from death. With my life more complicated than ever before, I began going to church again, and I began to have an unexplainable peace about my impending court date. I continued to agonize over these bad guys who had hurt me, but I wanted to find that place in my life that I experienced that summer at the Christian camp. There was something about the change I felt when I prayed that prayer with that lady, before I started making all these unwise choices. I wanted that feeling and that place back. To be honest, the more I went to church the more I felt that place again. I was also finding out more about the One who snatched me away from the grips of death's valley and gave me a second chance at life.

One day I was in my car and low and behold I saw a familiar car ahead of me. Yep, the so called friend that had tried to kill me was within view. All this new peace in my life was put to the test. I know you, the reader, may feel I did the right thing and just let it go, but that would be where you go wrong. It was all that fury that had built up in me and just came to my mind. Without giving it a second thought, I reached for my gun, which I kept very near, and followed him. Then, as if some strange reason, I got caught at a light. The more I sat there waiting for the light to turn green and continue my pursuit, the more these thoughts played out in my head of what I was going to do and the best time to do it. Before the light turned green, I heard this voice and I speak no lie. It said, "If I did not let him kill you, what makes you think that I will let you kill him?"

I was flabbergasted, because all the justifiable thoughts, that I had felt about having to do back to this guy and that he deserved to be punished, left as these words pierced my heart. I just sat there with my gun on my lap until I heard all these loud sounding horns. Then I realized that I was sitting at the light that was no longer red and had been green for some time. I did not follow him anymore. I was a totally shaken up at what I had just heard. From that point on, I never pursued to kill him again.

I really was a changed person and for the oddest reason, I had someone keeping me in line. With this new change, I became more involved in church, and the more I grew to know Jesus. I even imagined that since I gave my life back to Jesus that He would see that I was found not guilty, as my court date was staring me in the face. Of course, I knew that was totally wishful thinking or just plain foolish. Nevertheless, I remember asking the Lord to keep me from prison, and I promised I would live my life telling others what He had done.

The court day came and I did not try to run away. The trial ended and as the decision was ready to be given, I looked out the courthouse window at the sun. It was as if the Lord said to me, "I will bless you going in and I will bless you when you come out." A peace came over me, because I had been shaking like a leaf waiting on the jury to give their verdict. I knew I would be found guilty and the reality of the matter was I was guilty. Being in possession and selling drugs is a crime and there are always consequences. Before the verdict was given, I reached in my pocket and gave my attorney my car and house keys and asked him to give them to my brother. He said, "Are you about to do something crazy?" I replied, "No, but I am pretty sure I am about to go to prison. Or as in Jonah's case, I was headed for the belly of the whale."

The jury looked at me and said "guilty" and watched for my reaction. I simply said, "Yes, your honor, I am." I mean, come on, I was caught red handed with $10,250 on the table and 18 ounces of cocaine in a bag by the confidential informant. Somehow I knew if the Lord had given me peace during this trial of the consequences of my old living, I was sure He would give this new man I was becoming the grace to get through prison. It was hard coming to grips with the fact I was going to prison and very unsure what was behind those walls. One thing I did know was that I would need the Lord's strength more than ever. I really was in the belly of the fish.

There were a lot of guys in prison who knew who and what I was. Somehow they had the idea that I was about to be their opportunity to make things happen inside the prison walls, because of my past connections. They were a bit amazed when I began to tell them about Jesus and how He had changed my life and about salvation and being saved. Of course, they were not interested but they did respect my choice. I found out very quickly that it was all about respect in that place. Naturally, they hoped this was a phase I would soon forget, and when the pressure was on, I would revert back to my past ways.

One day in prayer, I began to ask God, not when He would get me out, but what He wanted me to do while I was there. His answer came no less than a week later. This officer visited my cell and said that I had to go see the Chaplain. I thought nothing of this but wondered why. The Chaplain said, "So you are the one they keep telling me about." I was now quite confused and had no idea what he was saying. I said, "I am sorry sir but I don't understand why I am here." He began to tell me how some of the guys had said he needed to hear this man preach that had been preaching in the yard. Affirming to him that we had Bible study each yard period, I thought I was in trouble. We were not supposed to preach in the yard, but sometimes the particular officer on duty had no problem with it. The Chaplain went on to explain that men's lives were being changed and some were signing up for services. I couldn't believe he actually wanted me to come and work in the chapel with him.

Now I could preach all I wanted to without the officers bothering me. I thanked him and he told me that anytime I wanted to get out of my cell to pray or study, the chapel was at my disposal. Suddenly it became clear that the prayer, where I had asked the Lord a week earlier what He wanted me to do while in prison, had just been answered. At times we had a packed chapel of men that had broken all sorts of laws. There were murderers, drug dealers, thieves, rapists and others coming to hear what the Lord had to say. I would express to them, "I don't care about your face or case; I care about your heart and soul becoming whole and healed." You see many times people would look differently at a person, if they were not the same shade of color or had committed a different crime. I would tell them that even though the man's laws we broke were not the same, we all broke the same laws according to God. We needed to get right with God's law.

They used to tell me all the time that people had come to them in the past to tell them they needed to change their lives. They did not heed these people, but would tell me that with me it was different and they wanted to hear more. God began to do some pretty amazing things in that place. Let's just say I was not the only man snatched from the valley of death. These men were discovering their lives were meant for something far better. Even some of the officers or their family members would come to my cell and ask for prayer. I was told I didn't look like I belonged there. Many would ask if I would be preaching in the chapel on Sunday and hoped they would work that day so they could hear me preach.

Time was passing quickly and years felt like days. Nevertheless, I still had this natural life without possibility of parole. No matter how fast time was moving, I still had no proof that I would ever be released from prison. I admit I would be filled with doubt at times. Still prisoners and staff were being saved and having their lives changed. This was great, but I really wanted another opportunity to live outside those walls again. The years continued and my faith was tested by all these thoughts. I had to remember that God had been so patient with me during the bad years of drug dealing, so I must be patient that He would get me out of this place. *Hebrews 11:1 struck me one day: "Now faith is the substance of things hoped for, and evidence of things not seen." (NKJV).* There it was all the time, written in the Word, which I had to write on my heart. I continued to encourage and tell the men about the love of Jesus!

One glad morning I awoke to my miracle. The officer came to my door and said my counselor needed to see me.

I took my time as I figured it wasn't too important. Then the counselor appeared at my door and asked if I heard the news. I immediately thought something had happened to one of my family, because bad news usually came from your counselor. When he found out I didn't know this news, he asked me to come to his office. I knew then it had to be bad news, and I braced myself for his next words. He told me to have a seat, extended his hand and said, "Congratulations!" Not understanding what was taking place, I shook his hand and asked, "What for?" He replied, "You are going home." He had just received this information from the Governor's office that my sentence had been commuted. I began to ask was he playing with me and he told me no. The guys around the counselor's door, who were waiting to see him, thought I had just heard about someone dying in my family, because I had tears in my eyes. Little did they know, I had just received the best news ever. So many thoughts and emotions ran through my mind and heart. My body was in total shock, as the counselor explained what was about to take place and how fast they were moving to get me out of there. The sentence had been commuted to 16 years and 9 months; I had already served 18 years. I had obviously served more time than I had to serve, but I walked back to my cell a very happy man.

The Governor had spoken on my behalf, just as with Jonah, when his time in the whale was up, the Lord spewed him upon the land. My mind went back to the moment I was at death valley's door and how God had snatched me back to face prison, a prison I was never to escape from, and how God had shown me mercy and favor. In a matter of days, I would be free. I cried and shouted and praised God as I came to grips with the fact that God's sparing me through all the ordeals surely meant He had a purpose for me. At that point, I determined to let nothing get in the way of finding that purpose and letting the Lord fulfill it. Meanwhile, as I prepared myself to be a free man again, it was hard on some of the guys. They were used to my encouragement and teaching, and they felt a sense of peace when I came around them. Even so, they were happy I was leaving and gave me their best.

I can remember my day of release; it was June 8, and the officer called my name and said, "Free man on deck." I walked down the stairs and all the guys shook my hand and gave me a hug. They thanked me for never changing and encouraged me to stay the same. I even saw tears in some of their eyes. Then the officer came and led me to the gate. The most beautiful sight was that gate opening, and the officer saying to me, "You are free to go!!!!!!!" On the other side were my sister and Gary waiting for me. Gary, the same man who told me about seeing my dead sister again, the same man who took me to A.Y.F., the same man that took me to the summer Christian camp where I first gave my life to the Lord, was standing on the other side of that gate where I walked to my freedom. The first thing he said was, "God blessed you, son." That was surely the truth, because at that same moment, I heard that same voice as in the court house about blessing my going in and my coming out.

> *Deuteronomy 28:6 "Blessed shall you be when you come in, and blessed you shall be when you go out." NKJV*

God had been with me everyday of those eighteen years, just as He had been with me when my friend, Chris, was murdered and when I was in the valley of the shadow of death. Now He was ready for me to be with Him in this new debt free life with all the many gifts He allowed me to realize during those eighteen years. Spiritual gifts to minister to the men behind bars and help change lives for the better. Gifts to help them enjoy the freedom that Jesus gives us from the captivity of the devil. Like the words in Isaiah 61:1:

> *"The Spirit of the Sovereign Lord is upon me, for the Lord has anointed me to bring good news to the poor. He has sent me to comfort the brokenhearted and to proclaim that captives will be released and prisoners will be freed." NLT*

After the three of us shared tears of joy, the next words out of my mouth were, "I want to go to Steak and Shake." They laughed and asked me if I was sure. I said, "Just as sure as me saying it again." In prison, I didn't exactly get many choices as to what to eat and you pretty much ate what they served you. I would watch commercials on television and dream of being on the outside and going to Steak and Shake. When we arrived there, I was like a kid staring at the menu with my mouth half open, looking at all the pictures of burgers and shakes and fries. My sister sat there and cried because she had her oldest brother back, and she could see the excitement in my eyes.

Before leaving prison, I asked the Lord where I should live, if I were ever free again. I certainly did not want to go back to the same old places and the same old life. I trusted the Lord and moved south. I had plenty of old friends that would have given me whatever I needed, but the Lord had taught me not to trust in ungodly riches. Not knowing what the Lord had in store for me, this move south was where my twin brothers had moved about six years prior to my release. They were more than willing to support me, which I am glad to say were the same two young boys who stood by my mother's side and needed to be taken care of after her death, the same boys I used to check on at school with their teachers to see how they were doing; these same two brothers were now supporting me. It amazed me that this was the true meaning of family.

I was also amazed at the changes in the world around me. There were so many different restaurants and stores that I had never seen. It was as if God had used those eighteen years to wash me from my past, clean my slate, renew my life, and then give it back to me to live again without all the past memories. Everything I saw was new; I was brand new. Like the Bible says:

> *Matthew 9:17 "And no one puts new wine into old wineskins. For the old skins would burst from the pressure, spilling wine and ruining the skins. New wine is stored in new wineskins so that both are preserved." NLT*

> *Luke 5:36 "Then Jesus gave them this illustration: 'No one tears a piece of cloth from a new garment and uses it to patch an old garment. For then the new garment would be ruined, and the new patch wouldn't even match the old garment'." NLT*

The same as with my life, God took my eighteen years, building my new character, disposing of the bitterness and resentment of my mother's death, the pride of making so much money and buying everything I could except peace and happiness. I had separated myself from my family, trying to love them from afar. What they really wanted was their brother back and not all the things. They had to grow up without a mother and father and, thanks to me, no big brother. So God took those years and chiseled away the old man and then created this new man. He cleaned the slate from the past with a whole new look and change in the world. *11 Corinthians 5:17 says, "This means that anyone who belongs to Christ has become a new person. The old life is gone; a new life has begun!" NLT*

CHAPTER 6

FREE TO LOVE—THE PROVERBS 31 WIFE

John 8:31-32 "Jesus said to the people who believed in Him, 'You are truly my disciples if you remain faithful to my teachings and you will know the truth, and the truth will set you free'." NLT

John 8:34 "Jesus replied, 'I tell you the truth, everyone who sins is a slave of sin. A slave is not a permanent member of the family, but a son is part of the family forever. So if the Son sets you free, you are truly free'." NLT

Galatians 5:13 "For you have been called to live in freedom, my brothers and sisters. But don't use your freedom to satisfy your sinful nature. Instead, use your freedom to serve one another in love." NLT

The Lord placed me back in society to till His garden. He had to make me a man of God first, so that I could be a son to Him, a future husband to my wife, a father to my children, a brother to my brothers and sister, and a witness to all that are in need to know the truth. I was in agreement with all the Lord was doing in my life; however, I lacked a wife. The Lord knows the many conversations we had on that issue. I vowed when I was released that I was not interested in any of my past relationships, and I wanted someone of God's choosing. I remember God leading me to *Proverbs 31:10 "Who can find a virtuous and capable wife?" NLT*

Some of Biblical descriptions of the Proverbs 31 woman are as follows:

> *She is more precious than rubies.*
> *Her husband can trust her, and she will greatly enrich his life.*
> *She brings him good, not harm, all the days of his life.*
> *She is energetic and strong, a hard worker.*
> *She extends a helping hand to the poor and opens her arms to the needy.*
> *She is clothed with strength and dignity.*
> *Her words are wise.*

After reading that Proverb, I knew for sure this was my marriage application for a wife. God's Word had given me the complete format as to how she should be, and I was not settling for anything less. I was a new creation in Christ and had been set aside from fleshly desires for eighteen years, so I would be deserving of a wife like the Proverbs 31 woman. A prudent wife is from the Lord and I was awaiting her delivery.

I began to search for employment, never thinking this would be where I would find such a woman. My brother spoke with his coworker about hiring me and said I would be getting a call during the week. In the meantime, I was doing odd jobs around both my twin brothers' houses. One day I was painting my brother's outside window, and as I was headed up the ladder, my phone rang. I didn't think it was important so it kept ringing. When I reached the roof, it dawned on me that the call might be about the job. I saw that there was a voice mail message so I pressed for it to play. There was a voice on the other end; this is about to sound mushy, but the voice sounded like an angel. Maybe I had been locked up too long but that is the way she sounded to me. The lady said, "Hello, my name is Lorraine." That's all she had to say to melt my heart. She was calling to set up an interview and asked me to return her call. I have to admit I almost slid down the ladder so I could hear the voice mail again. I listened to that message about ten times.

"My name is Lorraine," There was something about that voice and name that I just could not shake loose. It was more like a deep move inside of my being that just leaped out at the name, Lorraine. Now don't get this twisted, because I had many ladies say their name while I had been out of prison, but never did any name move me like this. I hurried to dial back the number, and, when she answered, "Hello, my name is Lorraine" that same thing happened. I proceeded to give my name and tell her why I was calling. Before I could finish, she said, "Oh, I have been waiting for your call; I have heard so much about you." I wondered which part she had heard—the old or the new. She had heard both, and we began to talk lifting up the name of the Lord and how good He had been in our lives.

We talked about the things God had done and brought us through. I remember she asked me what it was like to be locked up for so long. I was not ashamed to tell her and it was as if we already knew each other. We finally got to the application process and agreed to talk more later.

I saved the voice mail so I could listen to it again. "What just took place?" I asked the Lord. What was supposed to be a job interview seemed more like an interview for a Proverbs 31 wife. I sure couldn't paint anymore that day. I was so unfocused on painting that I just left the paint can on the roof. Lorraine and I began talking a lot on the phone and the more we learned about each other, the more I knew she was a devoted woman of God. And here I was, a man of God, set aside for His purpose, just released from an eighteen year journey in prison, finding a relationship with no shame or judgment toward one another.

Well, I did not get the job, because of my past history and prison record, but I came away with something so much better. I came away with my Proverb 31 wife. I believe that voice mail on the roof top was God's message through Lorraine. That voice that touched me so deeply changed my life even more. We began to spend a great deal of time together talking on the phone and going out to have a bite to eat. Yes, as the Word of God says in *Proverbs 18:22, "The man who finds a wife finds a treasure, and he receives favor from the LORD." (NLT)*. On March 19, 2011, I obtained my blessing of a wife and favor from the Lord. She truly is the Proverbs 31 fulfillment to me. We are in love with the one, true God, and He has given us our garden to till. We are diligent to keep out any beguiling serpents that may try to separate us from our God or from each other.

I found a job and have received promotion after promotion, because of the work I have done. I have allowed the Lord to shine through me even at my work place. Lorraine and I have a blessed church home, The Victory Church, that we call family. To this day, I owe it all to that man named Gary, who took the time on that sunny day to tell me about Jesus, when I was fifteen years old. Jesus, the Son of God, is the Savior of my soul, the Lord of my life and the King of Kings. He is the one who snatched me from death valley's grip and walked with me for the eighteen years of my self inflicted prison consequence. As I obeyed Him, he led me to my lovely Christian wife, Lorraine, and this wonderful fold of fellow flock, the Victory Church.

I am glad to have shared this testimony of my life with you, hoping to reach, if not the many, then that one lost sheep out there that is trying to find the way to the fold. You may be without hope and feel you are at the point of no return or you may be struggling with bitterness and resentment at the loss of a loved one and blaming it on God. Perhaps you are in the pride of life, at the top, and there is nothing you can't buy or get with all your ungodly riches. I can tell you from experience that you have not come to grips with the fact that it is no good if you gain the whole world and lose your soul. Like the Scriptures say:

> Luke 9:25 "And what do you benefit if you gain the whole world but are yourself lost or destroyed?" NLT

> Matthew 16:26 "And what do you benefit if you gain the whole world but lose your own soul? Is anything worth more than your soul?" NLT

To those of you in prison, you may need to know that in spite of the consequences you are suffering, the Bible says you can be forgiven. Whether a murderer or a thief or whatever your crime may be, you can be forgiven. In the future if you are going to suffer, suffer for Christ's sake and not for something wrong you have done. It is my hope that this book, in some small way, impacts you and shows you that you can rise above all this. Christ does not have to forgive you, but He is willing to do it anyway. Risen and forgiven, He didn't have to do it, but He did it anyway.

I felt God gave me this poem after He snatched me back from death and placed me among the living.

D.O.A (Dead on Arrival)

I never thought it would be this way, until I heard the man say D.O.A. is what he said as I laid there upon my stretcher bed. All my systems shut down, man I never thought this would be the last time I move around. Getting closer to hell's gate, I heard another voice relate—Yea though he had done the worst but I have saved him from the curse. Death, that is, if you knew my next thoughts would have never been true if I was not alive to tell you. Jesus Christ spared my soul as my body laid there getting cold. Now my thoughts are turned around as my heart begins to pound. Now I can hear the man say, "Cancel that D.O.A., he's going to make it anyway."

Giving all glory and all honor to my Lord and Savior Jesus Christ, whom I say, "He didn't have to do it, but He did it anyway."

THE END

Printed in the United States
By Bookmasters